TOKENS

TOKENS

Contemporary Poetry
Of the Subway

Edited by

Peggy Garrison
David Quintavalle

P & Q Press, Publishers
New York, New York

Copyright © 2003 by P & Q Press, Publishers
All rights reserved. All works are copyright by the authors
unless otherwise expressed.

No part of this book may be used or reproduced in any
manner whatsoever without permission except in the case of
brief quotations embodied in critical articles or reviews.

Published in the United States of America by
P&Q Press, Publishers
PandQPress@aol.com

Second printing August 2004
Manufactured in the United States of America
by Cheetah Printing, Colorado Springs, CO 80903

ISBN: 1-893068-11-0

Acknowledgements

"*Intimacies # 4*", "*The Ancient Couple*", by Jeanette Adams, first appeared in
    Love Lyrics (Elmsford, NY: private, 1982). Copyright © 1982 Jeanette
    Adams and reprinted with her permission.
"*Début de Siècle*," by David Baker, first appeared in *Chelsea*. Copyright © 2001
    by David Baker and reprinted with his permission.
"*Beware*", by Linda Bosson, first appeared in *Plainsongs*, Vol. XXI, No. 2,
    Copyright © 2001 by Linda Bosson and reprinted with her permission.
"*Day Treatment,*" by W. E. Butts, first appeared in *Movies in a Small Town*
    (Mellen Press, 1997). Copyright © 1997 by W. E. Butts and reprinted
    with his permission.
"*Subway Safari,*" by George Drury, first appeared in *Strong Coffee*. Copyright ©
    1991 by George Drury and reprinted with his permission.

*Continued on p. 113, which constitutes
an extension of the copyright page*

Table of Contents

Illustrations

——————Jean Balderston

As the coin becomes a memory we celebrate the inspiration found in a city's subways. With or without tokens we travel beneath the surface.

The Editors

————Abdellah Akhdi

Subway Entrance

Green dome dripping, it squats
like an old bullfrog in the rain.

————Jean Balderston

To Bettina and Lilian

Intimacies #4

the women held each other
against blare of train
and stare of rider

The Ancient Couple
          (encountered on the D train)

good luck
pierced her ears green

many years handed him
a cane

songsounds of China
came between them
frequently

——————Jeanette Adams

In the Transbay Tube

In that tight-breath
body-heat way they
sit in silence as the train's
rumbling innards
tremble to a whisper.
They're stopped under
the bay and Macarthur is the transfer
point and there's not enough
time to catch the 70 anymore
and a row of gleaming
yellow taxis with bored
drivers sit along the crumbling
asphalt at the edge of someone's
thoughts.

Funny how strangers don't
talk to strangers and how warm a
friend's essence is next to you.

He'll be going back to Hong Kong soon
I will miss him.

—————Ren Adams

Nothing is more poetry
than the malfunctioning BART sign:

> THE STATION AGENT WHEN
> THE STATION AGENT WHEN

————Ren Adams

The Social Contract

One night while riding
the London underground
I watched a young man
(accepting what looked like
a friend's whispered dare)
strip off his clothes
and fold them up neatly
until he was left
with not a stitch on,
except for the boots
he'd had to remove
for just a short time
to get his jeans down.

There he sat
on his pile of clothes,
buck naked,
clean and muscular,
and with a nice smile.

All of us in that car
gasped first and stared,
looking him over
(some blushing, some brazen),
then, seeing he meant
and would do no harm,
we smiled back,
his friends now
and friends of one another.

And any time anyone
got on at a station
we turned in unison,
waiting to see

what would come next,
only to relax
when the stranger relaxed
and became our new friend.

Still, someone someplace
must have complained
to someone else there,
for at one stop
a uniform
appeared in the door
and ordered the guy,
but softly, politely,
to put on his clothes,
which he did
with no fuss,
and we went our own ways.

Yet while he was naked
we were joined together
in sweet solidarity:
it was all so innocent,
so civilized,
so good.

—————Jack Anderson

Début De Siècle

underground 4A.M.

No one on, no one off, no one around—
it's so late the train seems winded, blown in
on a pulse, pausing, the doorway bumping,
the eerie, warm recirculating air
of the loading area like an oil.
The light's the hospital light where a death
or a baby is waiting behind walls.

Inside, pane on pane is blued over with
posters of perfume nudes, poetry slams,
jeremiads to family values
no one reads, no one is going to read.
It's a short ride to dawn and the new day.
Under your seat, a boot, old butts, ripped books.
By your head, two dots of semen on the glass.

—————David Baker

martha and rose

two women waited for the subway
their names were martha and rose
martha was no more practical than rose was
neither one of them went to white sales
when they went shopping they bought ball point pens with
        plastic orchids on top
and gold-plated dialers for dialing their phones when
        they phoned each other at night
they didn't miss an evening
martha's princess phone was pink
rose's princess phone was beige
rose was the aggressive one
she always phoned first
martha always waited to answer until she heard rose's
        fourth ring
she liked to think of how rose was waiting at the end of
        the line
rose knew that martha would always be late for the subway
it cheered her to think of martha hurrying down the block
martha wasn't sure yet which saturday she was going to
        push rose off the platform
rose wasn't sure which saturday she'd push martha off
        either

————Jean Balderston

Ruggles Station

Two dogs, a white shepard and a shephard/lab mix. A woman
guides them onto the subway car. The woman next to me
wrinkles up her nose. *I can smell this one from here* she says.
Phew! The woman from across the aisle has two kids who
want to pat the dogs. *They're friendly to kids,* the dog woman
says.
*You have any dogs? Naw—I want to but we can't have
them where we're living. I wish we could! I always had
dogs growing up. I like your hair,* the dog woman says to
the girl petting her dog. *Looks awesome.* The girl smiles and
mumbles thanks. She wears braids done close to her head
with sparkly beads in them. The two women smile at each
other. Then a mother with a baby in a stroller tries to sit down
but the dogs are in the way so the dog woman says, *Here,
here, I'll make room for you.* Everyone is talking together
because of the dogs. The woman who turned up her nose
smells her fingers because she has touched the dogs and now
her fingers smell bad. I fish around in my straw bag, the one
from Shanghai, and find little foil packets of lemon scented
alcohol wipes, the kind my daughter loves to use to clean her
hands in remote places, like the subway. I hand one to the
woman and she says *Thanks* and tears the foil packet open
and unfolds the small square of moistened paper and wipes
her hands carefully and thoroughly. When I get off the train
at Downtown Crossing I turn back and see her sniffing her
hands. All day they will smell like lemon mixed with dog.

————Lenore Balliro

Beyond the Els

Like a mad Columbus,
I have been following the sun
beyond the edge of things.
East New York was my *shtetl* starting place.
It was divided, like Gaul, into three parts:
These parts were the Els: BMT, IRT, IND—
West, South, North, and the fourth direction,
The El-less dividing line: Crescent Street.
In my mind's vision, these demarcation zones
defined my poet's journey.
I had to seek what was beyond the Els.

Beyond the BMT (West) was Brokenland Brownsville:
Belmont Avenue's pushcarts, herring & pickle barrels,
chicken markets, the Amboy Dukes;
Junior High School 109;
Mrs. Amsham's embroidery class;
Mrs. Rubin's beginning Hebrew;
dear old Straus's anthem;
Mr. Flinker's discovery of my sulfur stink bomb in the auditorium;
the bridge over the train yards too dangerous to pass, but closer;
Grandma's gefilte fish, berry & peach & apple preserves;
barrels of fine dishes & family secrets;
Grandpa's auctions, treasure boxes bidding to be discovered;
Molly Picon's *Yidl Mitn Fidl.*

Beyond the IRT (South) was the Canarsie Dumplands:
My friend Goliger, "The Bug Man of Brooklyn,"
and our ritual search for cynthia and cecropia moth cocoons;
beetles pinned on Riker mounts; bicycles made from parts found
in the burning dumps; the water's edge; places to watch
          the submarine races.

Beyond the IND (North) was Strangeplace Highland Park:
High hills against the grain of wind & heavier-than-I newspaper
    load
to deliver in rain, sleet, snow, or hail; Jew-hating other newsboys;
servants' quarters behind the big houses of Mansionland;
    milkboxes; tips;
Italian groceries—long loaves of bread & cheese & sausages.

Beyond Crescent Street (East of Eden?) was Queens &
    the Long Indian Island:
Jahn's huge banana splits; girls from other planets;
Rego Park; my brother's teenlove, Diana; country in a city;
Mom's pre-Fuller Brush & Avon sales places:
Cutchogue, Hauppauge, Patchogue, Yaphank—
all the way to Montauk Point, the edge of Paumanok.
All these odysseys I took before I flew to Miami—
to that edge of America to learn about the Other Half at the hotels
where Abe, my father's friend, gave me entrée.

My journey's been from East New York to the World.
But always I return to basketball games in Howie's backyard;
stickball on Georgia Avenue with my huckleberry gang;
snowball fights over the ice dunes of '47;
banker-broker nut games in Passover spring;
turdpiles over the tar-coverings of the rooftops
where Blackie, my dog, did his summer duty,
where I would venture and spy the tiger lilies
growing in the gardens of my neighbors' patches of sky & hope,
where I would be Jimmy in his own little room again
when the blue birds would be over the white cliffs of Dover.

—————Stanley H. Barkan

Train Trouble

All the years I rode the subway solo
from Richmond Hill to Bay Ridge, where
Carmen waited, or to the Village,
where school and work resided, all
those late nights back from parties
or the graveyard shift at the Daily News,
(when Uncle Louie could get me on)
I never once was hassled by anyone
but cops: a sarcastic response
to my guileless request for directions
to the IRT; a command that I get my butt
off the steps (the benches were crowded,
and I was tired); a wake-up shake
on the 2 AM "A": "Where ya headed, chief?"
"Huh, what?"
"Where ya headed—ya miss ya stop?"
"No, I'm taking it to the end, Lefferts Blvd."
"Well, keep your head up, get me?"
Later, my older brother, a Narc himself,
told me the man was just watching out for me:
one style of muggers specialized in subway
sleepers, going through their pockets,
only cutting those who awoke to protest.
Still, I slept a hundred times before
on the subway, dozens times more after
and the only cut I recall—
that wise-ass who asked me did I know how to read,
his billy-club insulting my shoulders before
pointing to the sign for the #2 train,
speeding me away from his public servant
sneer, defining forever how safe I'd feel
whenever I'd spot
a transit cop.

—————Joe Benevento

That Which We Ride, We Ride

The 1/9 local on Christopher Street.
My station.
My place
in the New York City world.

The number 1 or 9 boldly emblazoned
on a red circle, as if this line
held the gamut
of passion-filled possibility.
And it has for me.

From here I have taken more than rides
from one point to another.
From here journeys have begun.
Had Ulysses been a Village dweller
he would have called his men to this
very station.

They would have peered
into the subway's dark tunnel.
A horizontal abyss with tracks.

On the downtown side,
I walk to the end
of the platform,
the front end,
wait for the
approaching light.

I stand there, close to the tracks
so I can see the train slow and
slow and right before it stops
I close my eyes so that memories
of past trips remain.

I like to hold the rail and stand.

The subway starts.

I look through the front window.
Wide-eyed now.
Facing the darkness.
Moving forward.
Plunging.

—————Adam Berlin

An Ostrich in the Subway

I saw an ostrich in the subway,
lanky and gray, holding on with its beak
as the straphangers scowled into papers.

When the train stopped at Wall Street,
the ostrich stepped off with its briefcase
and mingled with the gray multitude.

The other passengers stayed on
until they got to Coney Island
and buried their heads in the sand.

Alternate Route

"At night and on weekends your train may
run on routes it never ran on before."
　　　　　—sign at a New York subway station

Sometimes, when the moon is so full
that it almost bursts,
your train will rear like a stallion
and crash through the roof of the tunnel
and rumble its way up the side of a building
and shatter in thousands of pieces.
And you will be flung to the farthest recesses
of limitless space. You will never again
set eyes on the people you love,
though sometimes on the clearest nights
they will look up and see you twinkle.

————Linda Bosson

Beware

"Tuck your chains inside your clothing.
Keep your bracelets and watches out of sight.
Turn your rings around so stones don't show."
          —subway safety poster in New York

Tuck your chains inside your clothing,
and wear expensive garments inside out.
Turn your rings around so stones don't show.
Dismantle your watches.
Paint your gold fillings navy-blue.
Swallow your necklaces.
Shave off your hair.
(Wig makers are on the prowl.)
Leave your internal organs at home.
(Stolen body parts command high prices.)
Have a nice day,
and thank you for riding New York City Transit.

————Linda Bosson

People on the Train: Overview

—————Ryn Gargulinski

Rush Hour Inside the Train

————Ryn Gargulinski

Uncross

We were jabbering away as usual
on the subway,
crossing and re-crossing our legs
buttoned warm in our coat of words.
Through the metal doors between cars
crossed a man on crutches.
A knapsack dragged from a shoulder.
He was one leg.
He hopped past us,
stopped and turned to my eyes,
held out a beaten coffee cup.
I uncrossed my legs
and reached into my pocket:
a token and a quarter.
I dropped in only the quarter.
"Thank you." His eyes
were already on someone else.
I re-crossed my legs
without thinking
because I could.

————David Breitkopf

Dislodged

in the aftermath of passion
I dream for my first time
in clumsy Russian.
I ask directions of another weary
middle-aged woman waiting
by the glow of chandeliers
beneath a mosaic-studded
vaulted ceiling in Komsomolskaya
Station of the Moscow Metro.
Pointing to a map, she speaks
to me in the familiar form, so perhaps
we are not strangers. I am unsure
if this is the beginning
or the end of my long journey.
Her voice is warm.
Ty zdeys', she tells me
in an awkward literal translation
of my native language:
You are here.

————Josephine Bridges

Day Treatment

At the top of the subway stairs,
eyes popping like an astronaut
who has just been unhooked,
he knows
he is a bright flash, then nothing.

He grips the railing like a child
making its first tentative way
through a terrifying new world.
He is like a man
with a gun barrel in his mouth.

I tell him not to be afraid.
I lie, and say everyone's safe.
This is what my work is,
to have the mind believe in itself,

even when it can't imagine a foot
descending down the next step.
I take his hand
and we go together into the screaming.

————W. E. Butts

Weird Subway Day

saturday afternoon
cusp of fall above
59th street station

underneath,
edge of chaos—
a loudspeaker voice
is trying to get the attention
of an invisible conductor
in a maintenance train full of asbestos
and warning signs,
stuck on the tracks

it's almost as though
chalky fumes killed the driver,
who's maybe passed out at the wheel
after hijacking the cancer

and me having just thought
I'm going to die early,
the only explanation
for my restlessness
(get it all in)
and the reason why
nothing you ever do
is enough

—————Charlotte Butzin

for the man on 130th

1.
You leaned into me, to rest, I thought, but you were trying to get my
attention. I wished you wouldn't touch me on the subway. Our date
started on Thursday. Sunday morning, on my way back to you, I
got off at the wrong station and came up on a block that looked like
yours but that I had never seen before.

2.
Days were short, dark by five. We ate breakfast at three, when we
woke up. I stuck my head into the light well and strained to see up.
Look, I joked flatly, the wind has blown the sky away.

3.
Having scrawled Thank You onto the cover of the Village Voice that
was under your sofa, I made myself hot tea for walking and poured
it into an old paper cup I found in your sink: leaving you sleeping on
your stomach. Without sleep a day is too much like the previous one.
My tea tasted of coffee and dried milk. I can see inside the trucks
that lumber past me, they're greasy and have an engine
trapped inside of them. I'll return your paper cup next time you
invite me
over.

4.
O sweet: our future was once our best kept secret.

5.
Sometimes I call you late at night, to interrupt your sleep. I listen to
the whole of your outgoing message, but hang up before the beep. In
this way I can be sure you have no record of my breathing.

———Jorge Ignacio Cortiñas

22

The Apollo Belvedere
Disappears
At Bowling Green

Out of dark rain strides a golden god disguised
in jeans and jacket faded slightly lighter
than eyes below bronze brows
drawn above arching lips.
Translucent nails tip fingers
as they grip the silver subway pole.
Quick parabolic inner thighs contract
to hurl him through those opening doors
launching him out across a crowded platform
an apparition moving—forever—into morning.

————Robert Crockett

Little Prayer

The platform smells like smoke. The Q-train's late.
The day is full of promises and dread,
with things to say, and things to leave unsaid;
with broken webs to mend or re-create.

The smaller comforts lift, but don't sustain:
the cat that soothes, the coffee cup that warms.
Oh, God, in both your male and female forms,
I ask for help to pull it off again.

I check the things I'll need: keys, schedule, face.
I cannot name myself. Can I name you:
craftsperson, landsman, poet, Buddhist, Jew?
Have you some power to lend? A little grace?

This is my little prayer, my subway prayer:
Please help me travel well from here to there.

—————Enid Dame

Subway Story #3: The Suicide

He leaps onto the tracks, won't
climb up, come when he's called.
He reaches for the third rail,
known to kill quickly,
but no such luck.
Women watching shriek,
run for help. Men step in,
grip his wrists, try brute force,
but he hisses *No, this life's
not worth living.* We're dumbstruck.
He'd prefer to burn than stay
among us, choose dark over day,
the underworld where traffic flows
all hours, slows at night but still
keeps going. First we feel spurned,
then angry as it becomes clear
the action won't run backwards:
he won't join us on the platform and wait
patiently for the next train, pretend
everything's okay, we're all
headed home somewhere safe.

————————Kathryn Daniels

Self Observation on the Subway

Eight indents in the reflective aluminum wall opposite me
turn my face into a series of screaming mouths.

I am a monster.

————Robin Dann

Subway Sight

In the overheated #6 uptown
a small boy in an overlarge jacket
stares forward with big dark eyes,
hair clipped close to his skull,
high forehead dome exposed,
legs straight out in front of him.
His mother, gold earrings shaking
in loud conversation with a friend,
absently pulls the boy close.
At her touch, his eyelids flip down,
he slumps into dream.
When she adjusts her position and shoves the boy upright,
his eyes pop open and he whispers, "Let's go home."
"Stop being smart with me," she snaps, and continues her
conversation.
Blank-eyed, the boy again tilts slowly toward her quilted arm.
At her glance, the boy whispers again, "I want to go home."
"NO," she spits like a hammer-blow.
His face a mask of unblemished bleakness,
head sunk into his narrow shoulders,
he faces the row of variegated subway riders,
unable to find sleep.

——————Nina Drooker

Subway Safari

When the modern hunter
saw the Safari Queen
at the turnstile,

he started
fishing,
and cast

his conjecture
her way.
She sounded

in the negative
and was gone.

He never got
another shot.

—————George Drury

Ghosts

You never hear them speak, but you see them.
Bill, whose heart exploded ten years ago:
a taller version of him folds *The Wall Street Journal*
lengthwise one morning, and though
you never saw Bill read the newspaper,
he would have folded it this way.
And Jon, released somehow from the ceiling of ice
over a March pond, stands warm and intact
on an elevated train.
Charlie, the laughing man who called himself
Sweet Chocolate, sells incense in a Queens subway station,
but he wears white linen now, and healthy flesh
fills out his round cheeks.
You keep forgetting they found Pete slumped
on a bathroom floor; you swear you see him drive by
with the windows down, singing and shirtless.
And Jim, whose shoulders filled your doorways
all those years, appears on the #7 one night,
his right temple without blemish, he is turned
toward the black window, he pays you no mind at all.
You see them. They live in cities. They change.

—————Lonnie Hull DuPont

El Exchange

In this cabin of convergence we are a moving ganglion,
agendas wound and pulled across each other
like threads knotted in the fingers of God.
What if all these trajectories altered slightly by proximity
or crossed and exchanged inside this bound tangle of life
and I found myself at the clinic for the pregnancy test
of the pensive young girl in black
and couldn't feel which news to rejoice at?
And the musician there with the dreaded hair
appeared in the high rise corner office
of the guy standing beside him
(one hand holding briefcase, the other on the rail)
to rest his dented sax on a stack of mail?
And *he* kept the rendezvous with *her* lover
only to discover something new? And that
boss showed up for this girl's interview?
And the graying gentleman in three piece suit
would arrive to clean the plush condo not knowing
where they kept the oven cleaner or the Sani-Flush?
And this woman sat in that girl's chair
in philosophy class not having read the Kant
while the well-prepared girl,
plunked down in a stranger's office,
were unable to show new clients what they want,
and *he* found himself telling that man's therapist
the secret of his deepest dread?
And this boy beside me wandered
in a strange apartment groping for the bed?
And what if the old man in the corner
were to find this poem unwinding in his head?

————Maureen Tolman Flannery

nocturne #20

black attache
beside the bench
on this el platform
you sigh the heat of five o'clock
valise sub luna
not yet lost and found

————Adrian Robert Ford

————Robin M. Glassman

B Station

Christmas Eve,
standing on the platform,
I watch an A train tear
        through snow,
        send sparks on the street.
Night is black, and people
        inside blur
        into peach and pepper
        ribbons,
letting brilliance.

—————Cynthia Gallaher

A Subway Ride in New York
                (after Ginsberg)

42nd Street, rush hour, I push my way onto the downtown local and squeeze in next to a middle-aged woman—short black hair, black dress, not attractive but stately. "You look like Gertrude Stein," I say under my breath.

> "Am I am or I yes," her firm answer.
> "Ms. Stein, why do you write in riddles?"
> "Riddles riddle Ritalin to ridicule."
> (I have to admit that makes sense.)
> "But it makes you almost unreadable and that irritates me because I know you're saying something important."
> She looks at me thoughtfully and says, "A read is a reed."
> "And how could you be friends with that horrible Picasso?"
> "Extremes open seams and friendship should never less seem."

Then her voice turns tourist as she asks, "Please, can you tell me if this train bridges Brooklyn or must I train change?"
The white tiles and the beavers—my stop, Astor Place. I train the get off, bow low and thank her for *Melanctha*.

————Peggy Garrison

Orpheus Meets John Weiners on the Subway in Boston

I get on at Central Square.
I see John Weiners sleeping there.

Last train to Park Street.
I notice John's wrapped in a sheet.

I nudge him a little.
"Hey, man. Wake up. Live a little."

"Wow. How y' doin', Orphee?
This the train t' Braintree?"

"There ain't no train t' Braintree. This goes to Park."
The lights go out and it's like fuckin' pitch dark.

Cerberus pads up the aisle,
stops in front of us and gives us a smile.

"Save me, Orphee!
The Dog from Hell is smilin' at me."

————John Gilgun

Subway Pocket Poem

Four middle aged men enter the car,
hard hats in one hand, flashlights
in the other. They wear white
and orange striped slickers, drop
into seats without words. They sit
with legs spread, heads back and eyes
shut. I watch lines of sweat slide
down their necks. Broadway-Layfayette.

Three of them nod, get off.
The fourth hunches over, reaches
into his back pocket. Fingers unroll
a lean magazine and his eyes become
lit trees on Christmas Eve as he flips
through glossy pictures of electric trains.

————Tony Gloeggler

Windows

On graveyard shift
those December nights,
riding the BMT above-ground,
midnight voyeur,
nose pressed against the pane,
I peered into rooms ablaze with Xmas trees
pretending I was that woman
handing someone a drink
or smoothing the hair of her child,
or smiling complicitly at the man touching her arm,
imagining even the smell of pine...
until the train descending
into blackness
burrowed into the earth's caverns,
and in the dirt-smeared window
I saw reflected back
only my vacant stare.

——————Eve Goodman

In the Subway

Often I want to move back
to a place where all trains stand still,

but I've just arrived in this city
(does it rain here only on weekends?)

whose streets lead to the underworld
full of ghosts reading magazines.

I am its single resident.

There are no other cities.

———————Piotr Gwiazda

Extinction of the Species

I carry my own museum of art inside my head. My face
reflected in the aluminum wall of the subway car is a cubist
painting by Picasso and I feel like a self-portrait by Frida
Kahlo, the one called "Without Hope." Outside the window
black crows by Van Gogh perch on top of wooden water towers
of old factories that line a deserted Edward Hopper street.
The passengers on the train look like a collaboration between
Otto Dix and George Grosz. An old crone from the "Carnival"
by Max Beckmann begs for coins, but everyone ignores her as
the subway speeds forward into a monochromatic landscape
titled "Extinction of the Species."

————Steven Hartman

Spenser on the "E"

On the uptown "E" I meet McElroy,
the great novelist (also a great guy),
and we swap news, about his wife and boy
and new story, about my sonnetry,
and Joe says, *Why not give Spenser's a try?*
But, says I, *Spenser's form is short on rime—*
the sonnet's hard enough, but his rimes five
sounds, not seven, like Wm. Shakespeare's kind.
The Spenserian would stress out my mind,
like laboring over a Rubik's cube.
Slant the rimes, says Joe. *It's a breeze, you'll find.*
That's what goes down when writers ride the tube:
Serendipity sets down the challenge,
And our imagination must oblige.

——————George Held

Subway Pastoral

I have never used a compass, but when the wind
pushes the flap of a cigarette box the train
is two stops away.

I have told time from the sun only twice, but when light
moves along the track like long blond arms I say,
this is it.

I have never spooned soil with my thumb, but the sound
of an unclasping buckle, then the four beats
of a metal drum means the first car is about to emerge.

I have never hunted, but it takes
one hundred and eighty-three steps to walk the field
of this platform, sixteen steps

to go up this staircase, seventeen
to come down. The wrong train
has come twice

in my direction; the right train
three times, in the opposite and I have had visions
of car wheels and buses

and standing on the corner of Union Square with my hand
lifted in the air. I hear the squawk
of a turnstile above me and I want to say,

Sit by me, and when the N train arrives,
don't leave. I am waiting for the R.

————Corie Herman

The 6 Train to Whitlock Avenue

is familiar as a hiking trail--the one
where there is not a branch or root,
a strap of grass, a shoulder-like stone

to take hold of. The one with the incline
where I know to bend my knees, unbuckle
my spine, and unwrap my scarf

from my neck. The one where water
drips from loose ceiling rocks
at the Longwood stop. The one

with the pass where there is too
much mud to secure my footing, or
fix my staff into the ground. Each morning

I am close to falling. Each morning
I make it to where I am going.

——————Corie Herman

Motion
        —for Milton Kessler (1930 – 2000)

I know you had a poem plastered all over the Tube and you really
loved that Milt and frankly I did too both the poem and the idea
and in fact I've blown that poem up well my Lizzie did it for me as
a present: there it hangs above my computer "Thanks Forever":
but Milt the Poetry in Motion in NY is sponsored by Barnes &
Noble and all I've seen so far is Tennyson's "The Eagle" which is
okay I guess if you don't mind mixed metaphors but mostly I stand
when I ride and watch the car ahead of me: the car ahead Milt
you ever notice it floats positively buoyant on the track and you
know how crazy some of these conductors are pushing 40 or more
on the straight-aways so the sparks light up the tunnels blue and
you see for a flash all the fat-font graffiti as foreign and urgent as
hieroglyphs: there you are bulleting along and the car ahead looks
any second ready to wrench itself free of the tracks and in the rich
fulmination of freedom crash and kill itself you know it's coming
you can see it the car jerking itself to every edge of the passage it's
coming a catastrophe worthy of NY: but in my car Milt it's like I'm
not moving at all it's like I'm riding in a subway movie-prop sure I
have to move a foot now and then but that's it one foot and not even
a lot: even though intellectually I know my car *must needs* be doing
what the car ahead of me is doing and remember that car ahead
is doing everything it can to derail itself but Milt in my car I can't
feel it I see it in the car ahead but I just move a foot a little now and
then: I see it but I can't feel it Milt it scares me how little I feel

————Carlos Hernandez

At the Subway in Grand Central Station

the talent is out of this world!
And Times Square is a good stop too,
and Port Authority, if
you're taking the A, C or E.

I saw a man, you wouldn't believe
what he could do with his life-size
woman-doll wearing a sequined salsa g-string
under her whirligig dress!
Her feet were velcroed to his shoes,
her hands were sewn together around his neck,
he'd tied his hands to her hips,
and Milt they danced nose to nose.

It was funny to watch, sure, but
it was no joke, the transfer of life
going on: the beauty of it came
in his utter surrender to the doll,
how she was leading him around,
like she knew that to make the tips she'd need
to show a little ass to the men in suits
and the high school boys who'd stopped to watch
for more than just a second. She knew no one
would stop to watch a man dance by himself—
she was dominant, aggressive, probably
she yelled at him at night in their apartment,
berating him for dancing badly as he
cleaned up the kitchen after dinner,

then made him beg for sex—which she
enjoyed more than he did. You can
tell a lot about a couple
by how they dance; you just knew
she whispered to him as they salsaed,
neither breaking their smiles for a second:
"You dance like a toad. Without me
you'd die of starvation."

————Carlos Hernandez

Manhattan Community College

In my stories before the bell
the I think Japanese man who claims the seat
by inserting his briefcase in an almost sexual
way, then squeezing in, takes out his long blue
cigarettes (it is obscene that they are not joints),
taps on the packet, lights one, then
gets out his disgusting brush. His hair is braided
in spidery chains leaving bald stretches.
At this I rise, and he says, "Look
lady, there is shit on your dress. See."
Standing till 59th Street I had looked down
on the eyelids (faint blue), the spidery lashes
of eyes protuberant like mine. No chin.
The face ending in the bottom lip. Red stockings,
white slacks with cummerbund, red blouse, black
skin. This thin girl in her pert Christmas way
before the door could close
had a cop knocking at the window at his braided head
and the man out on the platform at the end of a long nightstick.
So I come to you, —Yvrose is like a red rose
in a white eyelet blouse, cheeks incarnadine, the roster
aglow with Daffodil, Altagracia, Daisy Rivera, Maria deJesus.

————Jill Hoffman

46

City Subway

A family of refugees enter
burdened with bags and boxes,
bright weather-darkened faces.

I jump up making room, it seems
so right for them to stay together.

The little girls in flowery skirts
swing their legs, dark eyes dancing.
They speak softly like songs.

The grandmother, black bandanna,
thread-bare coat, raises her hand
to me like a blessing, bestowed.

I have done so little and yet
a glow of warmth feels like an
embrace from a continent away.

————Pud Houstoun

————Rosalyn Sandra Lee

like upski said...

they attempted to rob us of the subway trains,
buffing our paint and our pain
off the sides of brains,
where we labored intensely,
spelling our names
our own way,
trying to finally have our say,
cause I can't afford tv spots or billboard lots or radio talks.
but I can afford a can of paint,
so they lock that paint behind glass,
ask to see my i.d. and eye me warily.

they may have stolen our trains
but our hearts remain the same
and instead of dying out,
we are branching out like the rooster tree,
infecting every corner of this city,
so that everyone walking down the street
will have to see my name
my pain
and there are so many of us,
someone is going to have to listen,
as we rattle the bars of this prison.

————walidah imarisha

Little Dutch Boy

Waves pummel the sea wall.
Water rises behind eye sockets.
Will the stone in my face
hold back the sea once again?
As a trickle begs release,
I think of the Little Dutch Boy
in that story heard as a child,
that quick-thinking Dutch Boy
who plugged the dike
with his thumb.
Does he live in my ear?
Who stops each leak
from eroding the stone?
Father and mother buried
nine months apart,
I cannot cry
like the girl in the aisle seat
with fifty people on the train.
She hiccupped between sobs,
accepting tissues for ten stops.
How do drenched cheeks feel
when they dry?
Like sunshine after a flood?
If I stopped the Dutch Boy,
let the village wash away,
would I feel the
sunshine once again?

——————Jacqueline Jules

The El

I can not remember
their order any more.
When the trains came out of
tunnels at Utica,
was it Saratoga
or perhaps Rutland Road,
Rockaway or Junius,
then Van Siclen and home?

My early larceny—
a gum machine, its glass
face smashed (not by us).
We stood on the platform
and punctured holes in the
penny prizes with our
protractor points, sliding
them out with guilty joy.

In winter, stoves in front
of the change booths kept us
warm, until a metal
flap fell and announced the
coming train's arrival.
Winter was so cold
on that frozen platform
ice teeth hung from metal.

In summer the boys played
punch ball under the el.
And sometimes the hard hit
ball sailed over the
roof landing on the tracks.
The heat sweat the steel
and made the girders cry
when lethargy set in.

On the way home from school
on crisp autumn nights, one
could see the stars shine on
the dark empty streets of
all the homebody folk.
Back from the city on
the bundled winter nights,
the over heated car

made us sleepy and we
drifted to the rocking
wheels, our books beside us.
The El was the place to
be, the subway dull and
boxy. As a child
I slept a half block from
its rattle and never

heard a thing. And on my
corner the powerhouse,
lines of turbines feeding
all the movement, its big
brick wall a spaldeened field.
That metal El platform
was the thing for me, cool
under its shadows in
summer, rocking its old
mysterious reasons.
Gone from my sight, but seen
until the end of all.

—————Stephen Kaplan

To the Paris Metro Pickpocket,

dinner is on me

————Kit Kennedy

A Prayer to the Subway
                    (excerpt)

Our Father lost forever underground.
Our Father forever hurtling though sight and sound.
Our Father of the lumbering BMT.
Our Father of the slashing IRT.
Our Father of the savage IND.
Our Father of the painful and dull-witted crosstown shuttle.
Our Father who takes us screaming into the darker neighborhoods.
Our Father who slashes like a silver knife through the flirting
          stations.
Our Father who penetrates where we do not go for fear.
Our Father who purifies every layer of the dirt-caked girders.
Our Father who caresses every form slouched against the darkened
          walls.
Our Father who knows by heart every letter of the blood-red graffiti.
Our Father who dares to stop where we do not.
Our Father who knows the passage from dark into light.
Our Father who knows the voyage from despair into hope.
Our Father who knows that the human soul can never have any
          color
Our Father who doesn't fear the great elongated stations of our
          darker brothers.
Grant us freedom from the hatred of our skins.
Grant us liberty from the divisions of our hearts.

————Thomas Krampf

Two on the 2

Racing the length of the subway car,
he barely pauses to ask,
"Does this train go to 55th Street?"
A slight figure,
a guarded glance,
bare ankles,
no coat.
"How many stops?"
Others sit
        faces averted,
                blank,
                preoccupied,
                disinterested.
He pauses
caught by his reflection in the window,
adjusts the hooded sweatshirt
                framing his face

checks his pants slung low
                over narrow hips,
cuffs tucked into
scruffy hightops.

Suddenly, he runs and leaps again,
down the subway car.
Look at me...
feet pounding,
hands reaching.
Watch me... I *can* do stuff.
Pay attention. I exist!

————Joyce Kravets

The Bottle

The bottle hits the floor
and begins to roll.
We all look,
each eye checks to make sure the others do not see,
but the bottle sees all.
As it rolls
through grit and mud,
it captures all of what is left of everyone on a rainy Friday night.
Bumps against an ankle,
gets no response.

As I leave the train,
the bottle does not turn,
nor wander or ask,
but continues to bop its cap on the aluminum posts
and no one will look.

It is a shame
loneliness is the disease we fear,
laughter the joy we abandon,
and in the middle is where most of us lie,
watching the bottle roll by.

—————Otis Kriegel

Manhattan

A subway train vibrates
underground,
its sound the insistent
reminder of a city, its arms
those of an octopus. A
quick learner, like the mollusk,
it has a knack
for adaptation, can even
fade into the surroundings
at will, its suction cups
the many buildings taking
hold, moving the feed
to its mouth. It seems to
go great distances without
ever really leaving home.

————Donna J. Gelagotis Lee

From a Rooftop in Brooklyn

I join the subway as it rolls
toward Coney Island Beach,
legendary stops of the 50's,
where summer was a stroll
along the city boardwalk,
hot dogs at Nathan's, hands
gooey with the syrup
of a sprawling nation.

Today, a sea of flat brick
buildings combs

the grey air,
green parks pushing them
aside, schools still
straining to meet
the goals of a touchdown
democracy. Silver birds
cluster like butterflies
as they eagle-sweep through the
land they know, past faceless
windows, a country
underground.

But from here,
the boats of Sheepshead Bay
never move,
never glide over a slate
of grey-blue, as if they were anchored
to a picture post-
card, to a time when making the best
of it was not the snaking transport
in and out of a night's
boxed lives.

————Donna J. Gelagotis Lee

The Passenger

a child in a superman costume
is teetering on the edge of a Brooklyn roof
as the elevated m train i'm on passes by.
i mutter in passing,
    "don't try..."

————Donald Lev

The Woman on the Metro

She's nearly not from here, her old fashioned sneakers, jeans. She
is plain, chubby, from some small town I think. A 1970's jacket.
she's unlike the women in suits and sneakers buried in paper or the
men with *The Post*. She sprawls over the side seats as if on a sofa
in the sun. Between Vienna and Foggy Bottom I watch her start up
conversations with anyone who sits near. "Where are you from?"
and "What work do you do," she blurts in such an un-Washington
way I half expect the people she tells *her* story of being out here
from the state of Washington for a woman's conference to start to
move to another car, figure she's got a con, wonder what she is after.
But within moments, a blonde woman has invited her to church
and after the shock of having her quiet time interrupted, seems
almost ready to invite this woman home. "Are there many colleges
in Virginia," the visitor asks. When this woman gets out a stop
before they can exchange, numbers, though they do give each other
their name, she asks if any presidents were from D.C. I expect next
she'll wonder about inches of rainfall, average temperatures and
wind. When a black man sits near, she asks him if he's had a day of
stress and he looks at her oddly. I wonder if she's a Scientologist, in
a cult. She asks if he wants the paper near him he says, "It's sic of
one, half a dozen of the other." She's puzzled, confused, asks him
to repeat that, explain what he means. After he decides she's not
harassing him, he puts his paper down and they talk for a few stops.
He's from Arizona, commutes every two weeks and seems, in the
end, amused, not annoyed by her. The next woman is several seats
away but the woman, Annie, she tells everyone, "call me Annie,"
gets the text book she's reading for a course, who did her hair, what
soup she likes best. This isn't like many metro rides I've taken and
I think of how strange Shakers first seemed to me with their huge
cabbages and their chairs up on pegs and then how I got to admire
them. The last man looks like he definitely thinks she is strange.
He could be a burglar or on horse. With his baggy jeans and sullen
look, he seems startled when she asks if he's got a big family, if he's
in sales, does he like computers. He's the least willing to open to

her bland chit chat, gives a few yes and no answers and then looks like he wished he had anything, a phone book to bury himself in, another seat he could slink to but as he leaves, I see him smile. I can't imagine anyone less like me and I think at least I didn't get caught in the whirlpool of talk about things I'd never talk about and as she gets off for the Mayflower Hotel, I'm almost a little sorry I kept so well hidden, camouflaged behind my anthology of 1996 best books.

————Lyn Lifshin

Subway Fantasies

It begins with his face,
his shoulders, the way he carries himself, perhaps.
Clothes don't *always* make the man.
The slant of his jaw reveals confidence.
Intelligence shows in his eyes.

The softened edges of kindness and humor
emanate from his total demeanor.
He has the patience of a good lover, though
there's an immediate sense if this is *not* true,
rather than any confirmation that it is.

His hands can be rough,
but must evidence a gentle strength.
The chapped knuckles of a well-loved man
are not a deterrent
to a woman's breast.

I rarely notice what book he's holding
and usually select one who, like myself,
gazes transfixed in distraction.
I will him to look at me,
averting my eyes demurely when he does.

I choose one or another each night,
imagining we'll exit at the same stop and
go home to my kitchen to cook pasta
before making love.

It gets me through the day.

————Susan Mahan

subway

night in the station
    small lights in the wall
        day breaks
       into places
           to move toward

————D. H. Melhem

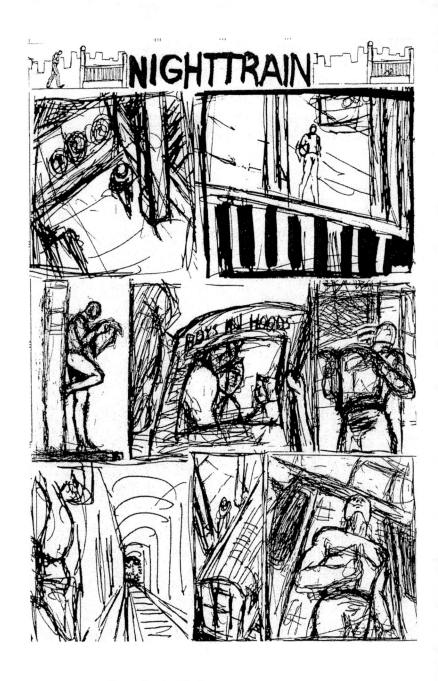

————Jose Luis Mojica

Miss Subways

Way back when, in the Forties and Fifties
Miss Subway's photo was hung in the trains.
She wore the usual little white blouse
with a Peter Pan collar, all-American
paradigm of the girl-next-door
any boy would take home to mother.

Nowadays she might sleep in the subway
(like sleepers in London during the Blitz.)
Sometimes she hangs out on Eleventh Avenue,
someone's teen daughter in satin shorts,
fishnet stockings, and four inch heels.
Hello sailor, new in town, she says.

Wanna party, wanna date, she says.
Sometimes she gets into a car with a stranger,
maybe from Lodi, with a teen daughter at home.
She does her sad, sticky number again.
Sometimes they find her left out in the rain
like a soiled dolly, eyes staring blank

as buttons, someone's black-and-blue-eyed baby
gone, on a date with the angels.

————Gertrude Morris

The A Train

I sail home on crescendos
Straphanging, scale home
on wailing rails and shrilling whistles.
Look, man, one hand!
Now skate along smooth grates
Rockety rocking faster
Swacketing down the track
(O shrieking screamer streaming down)
Held swinging in the growing dying roars.

—————Lillian Morrison

Transience

II.

She writes to him while traveling the South East coast, en route
to Taipei Railway Station – *Passengers on a train seem so
preoccupied with sitting in seats facing the direction of travel.*
There are individuals who complain of motion sickness, when
unable to see ahead to a point of destination. Those unlucky
enough to face backwards sleep, creating diversion. Sunlight and
betel nut trees float past the window. Fragments of dreams make
their way across the countryside.

That night, a rock concert and the staging of the new year in
Chinag-Kai Shek Memorial Plaza. Recollections of Morgan Neiman
who described life in Sevilla as being "outdoors a lot." She imagines
boarding an airplane home, crossing time zones and meridians to
meet him again. In the morning, telecasts of celebrations in the
States. Times Square, a falling ball of light, and the tradition of
kissing strangers.

II.

One morning, I ride the El into the city. Businessmen crowd the
aisles with briefcases. Raincoats, umbrellas, sweat. I look up from
his letter long enough to rest my eyes out the window. In Kyoto,
it is tomorrow. *Haru,* the commencement of a new season. The
train plunging beneath ground, that shift from light to dark—the
speed of a single film frame. White faces reflected in the blackness
of windows, expressions softened by steam. The hour in which
I waken, the hour in which he sleeps. Life a dream, lasting until
death, where fears and regrets are as unreal as desire.

————Shin Yu Pai

Air-conditioning in the Grand Central Subway Station!

Where will this end?
This transubstantiation, this meddling
with the ice caps. As I wait for the No. 5 train.
While outside it's 95° in the shade.
Down here we're strolling home, patiently stalled
in the nave of this relief. An engine roaring

its wind above us, a formidable feat
in the endless canon of feats: measuring
the immeasurable, a gene's immaculate lace, a star's
perishable light, a neurosurgeon teasing
a wiggle at last from the patient's toes.
Where normally I sweat like a baker
among his loaves in this eden

of weedy scents, every crust of it bitten through
and bobbing between the tracks. As I stand
among the hands cradling paperbacks, loosened
ties and nodding stares lost in music. A cool
breeze in my hair—listening beyond the small light
of this moment, every shoulder of it
leaning home.

—————Brent Pallas

underground

waiting for the train
I trace names of traveling multitudes
deeply carved
on a subway bench
bolted in concrete

eyes chase
railway rats
chasing tails
over splintered tracks
along tiled walls
where brown water stain drips
are suspended in motion
like oil on asphalt

a soiled paper tumbles
to my feet:
"A man...three shots to the chest...Saturday night
Any information ...contact...N.Y.P.D..."

and the blast of the engine's horn
sounds a deafening alarm
warning tunnel dweller shadows to flee
before dim light is seen.

————Lance Peterson

The A Train

There is green, crunchy confetti of pulverized Heineken bottle,
torn notices for a Public Hearing/Reuniòn Pùblica;
six pale pistachio shells huddle where the linoleum
curves to meet the wall.

Riding through Brooklyn at 8 AM.

Passengers enter and leave at each station
and I rate them twice; for potential danger and for sex appeal.
Odd how some score high on both scales.

At East New York two white women and a man jump up
from a platform bench to burst on with their luggage.
I guess they are travelers going to JFK, but were on the wrong train.
Emotions pass across their faces like cloud shadows on a field:
anticipation, recognition, relief.

Horses trot around Aqueduct racetrack in the distance as
the train pulls out of the ground and round the turn to the
Rockaways.
A black man to my right has methodically tweezed
beard stubble from his face
all the way from High Street where he got on
to Howard Beach where I get off.

——————David Quintavalle

Dinner on the #6 Train

for Octavio Paz

1. All of the things we never shared that belong to us, as the exalted prisoners of our maze of sacred Otherness, I might confide in you over a 45 minute lobster dinner in the deserted racing dining car of the empty #6 subway train. Antonio Machado wrote, "When all I wanted was to sing, I was accorded the honor of living." Now Octavio, you are gone and I dine alone.

2. Newspapers litter the floor, surprising me in a surreal instant with the news of my own death. I am traveling at the speed of your image in motion in my brain. Beside the lost and found of our obituaries beneath my foot, I spy a Playbill for a musical that in the confetti of my reverie, I imagine Julia de Burgos cast in her role as the daughter of your Mexican Eve or the Indian Virgin, never mind her puertoricaneity, and Glenn Gould as the pillhead chief presiding over an Aztec empire, both, in the prime of their singularity.

3. Companion, cracking a red claw, the solitary stops have names as lonely as the "O" in Olmec and in Toltec silences. The stations upon entering Manhattan now, post-*Conquista* feudal Spanish and the numbered streets are named for the equations used in pyramid construction subdivided by a memory of the Bronx sun over City Island where gunfire and churchbells are simultaneous in a din that would have vexed you.

4. Was it the fire-god Quetzalcóatl-Nanauatzin who was the last to speak to young Chatterton outside his ghostless room, convincing him to sacrifice himself? He might have died twisted sideways in a light-soaked Mayan hammock serenaded to his death by doll-like siren *mariachis* made of corn husks, imported from across the hot treeless paths and *indio* streets by wealthy peasants with no ancestry and pockets full of artifacts for visitors who stalk their genealogy.

5. Outside the enigma that is only reality, the dense truths trick those who die as they live. A candied leaf, a palliative, a pre-Columbian wafer, sweet under the tongue of the wasting minstrel, bought in the siesta heat from the illegitimate daughter of La Malinche and Nietzsche.

6. We are the children, mysterious to ourselves, pale copper. Lost to the perfect mystic swimming hole within that deep crumbling well of natural limestone, the *cenote* of your zero,

The energies of our civilizations, subdividing once more, before they are conquered, treading naked in the water that will purify itself.

7. Pragmatism is an abstraction bleeding us,

And, out of nothing comes *la raza cózmica*, laughter, nothingness itself,

Because, we do not perfect them;

Because, like our gods, love is *hijo de nada*,

Like the "O" in Octavio, orphaned by a ring of stars.

——————Lola Rodriguez

lost again on old subways

i am lost again on old subways
at third avenue station the lights go out
the lunatic laughs
the lunatic who does not appear
until the lights go out
and i cannot see him
and i cannot see what he is laughing at
he laughs and he laughs
death is solemn
but suffering is hysterical
when it happens to others
the three fates the three stooges
torturing each other in the darkness
while the children laugh
until the lights go out and they are stuck
in their own nightmares
and he laughs at my fear
and i laugh at him laughing at my fear
because i am afraid not to
keep the lunatic happy
and i have paid my fare and i must journey
there is nowhere to go but where the darkness takes me
and i must get my money's worth
the doors will not open
i cannot depart at the home station
and i slip past my sleeping parents
under the bronx and over the bronx
and all the unseen passengers on this runaway train
are laughing and laughing
because we are afraid to stop
we are lost in the bronx
where guns will not save us
and the churches are closed for the night
and the candles lit for the souls of the dead
have burned out and the priests
have locked the rectories

and we are laughing too hard to pray
and we are laughing so hard we almost enjoy it
we have transformed we are the laughing commuters
of the i.r.t which never looked so good
though we cannot see it as it trembles on
through the night which does not stop
through strange territories where strangers lurk
in the shadows waiting for a few laughs

————w. r. rodriguez

About Surprise

In a proverbial flash it comes to me
how crude our
human rudeness is—

        Why it should surprise
anyone who's skinned out
a rabbit,
to realize how thin the skin is

on human conventions, how
astonishingly quick
the wrong look
                at the right guy on the subway

could put your
lovely gleaming
guts lolling into your own bewildered hands

is perhaps the truly
wondrous thing about us. Such innocence

as peering curiously
out of the tall grass

a rabbit might experience, before the flash.

————William Pitt Root

Interior

Adjoining rooms: uninvited guests simply arrive and depart
and depart and arrive and the order of all this
appears out there in the moment—whatever all this means
is up to you. Do you suppose that Maggy the Cat is alive?
Like a woman riding the subway who finds:

Where there is silence there is thundering noise
Where eyes are wide open there are eyes wide shut

      holding firm... drifting quickly

but what does she find in this chamber of reality?
but what does she hope to find in this chamber of imagination?

                            but what must any of us relinquish
in this space?

Suppose you stare and only stare & suppose what is before you in
this crowded subway car is the most significant manuscript you will
ever bear witness to?

————Sue Rosen

On the Manhattan Bridge

Light that plucks softly
at the cables
lays itself wanly in the car.

From a staggering hand
streams a wonderful sketch.

The slender red-haired woman
in the paisley-tan dress
poses herself
stretching from a pillar.
She dreams of her office mates,
her coffee ache
while you think about her virtue
and Vermeer.

————David Sanua

Transport(s)

The weedy lilacs line the viaduct
dragging their scent on the concrete walls.
Inside the subway car
only you can smell the metal dust
electric, unaware.

Facing forward with fast intent
you urge the motorman on
with thwacks on your strap.
He doesn't hear.

At an undisclosed location
the dispatchers doze.

————David Sanua

The Cockatoo

To catch the Long Island
Railroad to Ronkonkoma,
we descend into the hole
called Penn Station,
down the filthy steps
into a dim, medieval crypt
of black grease and peeling paint,
into the unyielding air,
heavy with machines and bodies,
into the cursing, the screaming of trains,
where the stainless steel urinals
look like the minimal art
in the galleries above our heads,
where the numb faces lift
their eyes as if toward heaven,
fixed upon the changing
marquee of track destinations.

A tidy little man,
unremarkable within the waiting herd,
with carefully polished shoes,
precisely combed hair
and shirt and trousers
that seem as if laid out
by his mother forty years before,
opens a small cage
frees a brilliant white
apparition, a cockatoo
and sits the bird
on a trash container lid;
they share an ice cream

without a word,
without an open hat
and a beautiful woman,
a child, and then a crowd
pauses, gathers and smiles.

—————David Sapp

Gold in the Subway

Brown-skinned, black curly-hair,
she's 30, maybe 35, and tall, lanky so
the chesterfield coat hangs good on her

though at first I don't see anything but gold
when the doors open on 23rd, her metallic
gold shawl streaming through the metal doors,

bringing the sun here underground, deep
down, not caring if she's brazen, that she blazes
light where it's never asked in.

Standing on the A train, riding gold on her shoulders,
she is a tree in April, a god this woman,
and her wrap praises the day.

————Myra Shapiro

Scene

There is too much misery
in this city
                too much
pain
A dream last night of trains
Trapped in the entrance
pinned
                My path blocked
by strangers
Too many of us forced
to breach
the same space

& yet   as I walk along
the street
I am startled by a tree
Its bare twigs
                full of
 bright red berries
As if someone had placed
them there
to decorate
                the morning

————Susan Sherman

tuesday

men with gloves
leave your vision
as you submerge

on the platform
a group of diamond-eyed slicked-hair jacks
with oddly sculptured facial beards
converse in alien tongue

a large woman slams her handbag
into your elbow
your funny bone smarts
"s'cuse me" she utters and doesn't look back
you decide not to forgive her

a sax blows just the other side of
a stairway somewhere announcing
a gush of hot steam which messes
a tie guy's hair
surprisingly he stops you
and attempts soliciting spare change

you cough up half
your hershey bar
and nothing more

a high school drop out spits repeatedly
at the tracks
a nun stands near perspiring
minds her business

an omen of air swirls down the corridor
like an unleashed doberman
when the rumble of train cars peg the volume meter
doors spread wide
you march through the threshold of
the spray-painted steel sausage link
along with the rest of humanity
a well-dressed elderly woman hands you
a fresh tulip and smiles
you nearly forget the stench of urine
until your next breath

you smirk
put your nose into a paperback
and hope the weatherman will be
wrong again

————Dan Sicoli

Subway Map

What catches our eye
on this stylized chart
is the puff of white
in East River's blue.
A cartoon balloon
from the mouth of Queens
declaring: "Rikers Island."
Nothing else appears
in that tethered cloud.

Surrounding City's
gray street grid
overlaid with rainbow routes
trains burrow through.

Crisscrossed stripes
leave this isle untouched.
Free of quick transit
it floats solitary, apart;
with only a name.

————Dan Sieg

Beach's Palace

In 1912 hard hats dug the BMT,
rough-stuff drudges with smoot-smudged faces,
hewn hands thick as stumps in upstate
timber fields, sludging rock and heaving earth
aside for NYC's new Broadway line
they stumbled into an underground paradise,
recently built, long forgotten:

A salon 120 feet long laced with peeling frescoes,
remains of ornate paintings, chipped candelabras,
dusty chandeliers, and in the center,
an enormous dormant fountain.

In 1870 zircon lamps blazed upon New York's finest
as they glided in on curious smiles, eager for a first journey
in the lavish underground palace where sonatas
soared from the lively piano to the sublime fountain.
A giant fan thick as the breath of gods
propelled them, inhaling them through a sleek
cylinder of metal and stone.

Within a decade the luxury-lined subway was gone,
prey of mob boss politics and indifferent millionaires.
When workers unearthed its extravagant grave,
the canary in its gilded cage began to sing.
Eyes wide as children, even the tough laborers
stood silently, caught in a vision left like tiny,
indelible handprints in the dust black burrow—
a vision that we might, even in daily travel,
embrace a gentler version of ourselves,
prize the journey more than the destination.

————Elizabeth Simson

Into the Station

Pacing on a brick brown brick platform
w/ pimpled yellow trim
craning neck past the edge
of the down town train trench
rumble shakes steel rail
shuddering mice to hiding holes
scampering grey hair against sooty rails
like deaf chameleons w/ hairless tails
red & yellow white lights
herald orange people moving machine
thundering under city & streets
blurred speeding windows
display glimpses of flooded fluorescents &
faces flashing onto retinas
seeking familiarity and finding none
cars career into slowness
then stop
turning on softened rubber soles
eyes seek space
 to sit or stand w/ in
calculate distance and time
'til the doors' signaling chime
glimpse glance scan
then turn & swiftly stride
boarding outbound train
bounding towards Jamaica Plain

————Ian Thal

Unexpected

Riding the number seven train
I noticed
an elegant lady
sitting
across
from me

She was dressed
in a fine silk black gown
wearing a necklace
of precious pink pearls
and a suede coat

Sticking
out of her
meshed beaded black hand bag
was
a silver
gun.

—————Vincent J. Tomeo

Annie Leibowitz Said

Annie Leibowitz said "the best part about having money is not
            having to
associate with the general public"

I read that in an old Vanity Fair someone left on the subway
covered in fingerprinted dirt

Don't read much, got no time, read the number of the arriving train,
the numbers on my watch

My grandmother signed her name with an "X"

Photographs mean nothing to me, my brothers sit dying beside me
in a purchased oblivion

Someone's making money

————Nikki Tommins

over-ruled withdrawn sustained

if colin ferguson
wrote a poem
what would it have sounded like?
could we have grasped it?
and would we have wanted to?
(honestly)
when he shot up that train
          (allegedly)
was it not
emphatic expression
                    (tacitly)
of Black poetry in motion?
each discharged bullet
each compressed trigger click
a fragment of a phrase
of that never written stanza
of that unheard
poem

silence

and if miles couldn't blow that damn trumpet
so sweetly and fiercely
and literally weave
hovering notes of poetry with it
avenues were closed
leaving a choice of implode or explode
would he not have (eventually)
taken that piece of concocted metal
and slammed every cracka face
in the place
that denied him a job,
or fucked with his money?
bloody

90

And you bets to believe
that disability was fucking
with colin ferguson's money...

silence

And we must ask (finally)
will a 200 year prison sentence
erase what's already been written
by mr. ferguson (withdrawn)
was it not colin ferguson (over-ruled or ruled-over)
who set off a bomb
on the 4 train (WITHDRAWN!)
was it not colin ferguson (Objection)
ditty boppin' into Mickey D's restaurants (Objection)
Riddling the sacred patrons? (Objection)
Venting day Trader discord & mayhem!
(OBJECTION!)
Pink slippin' rounds in the CEO's cranium?
(OBJECTION!!!)

All across the land
sea to bloody sea
re-bloodying already-bloody burgers and buns,
spraying even more dark.. gooey.. syrupy sweet
(explode?)
into those carbonated, blood-red, sugar cane, cherry
cokes!!!
reddening christmas cards and junk mail at post offices
all across..(boss)
all across..(boss)
america

withdrawn
withdrawn
withdrawn
withdrawn
withdrawn

Over-ruled by boss america
withdrawn into silence
POP!, POP!, POP!

    (BANG,BANG,BANG) SuStained...

————Meneba Obassai Tresk

The '66 Mets

The El rattled past the Unisphere, skeletal,
the gristly webbing of some sea creature
left to bleach in the industrial
rain of Queens. The World's Fair was over.
The game called, we were thrown together
hip-to-hip to convey the deep
disinterest of commuters in one another's
lives, staring hard into the abandoned
thoroughfares of the future, not speaking.
But breathing. And one fan sidled up
to nestle his mouth in my hair, his beery
breath swabbing one ear, stiff prick
pressed into the damp hollow of my back,
passengers packed around us, yet distant,
a crowd in a photograph, the couplings
not clear.   Until a small commotion broke
out, some guy with two boys in baseball
gear clinging to his belt
warning, *Back off, bud,* his palm against
the breather's chest, the onlookers
tense but making room as the express
drummed into Queens Plaza and the amateur
molester ghosted off into the gray,
steel anonymity of the girders.
                              Fifteen,
I was too dumbstruck to murmur thanks, still
too simple to grasp how desire
can bully the body, any body, that father
ashen too, knuckling his boys' bristly
scalps beneath their blue caps
as the doors hissed shut and the train
jerked away from the station

into the spattering April
drizzle, an outcry of sparks
bursting from under blunt wheels,
the long, frustrating season just begun.

—————Michael Waters

Green Line

We were on the Green Line:
a rare outing,
just the two of us,
our kids at Nana's,
our friends busy that night.
A red-headed woman sat behind us;
I remember that.
But where were we going?
The train suddenly stopped
between stations
and the lights went out.
"The T sucks!"
You shouted
in the safety of the dark.
The red-headed woman—
who snuffled as I recall—
knew it was you.
So did I.
And I understood
that the father of my children
was an asshole.

————Patricia Wild

The Yard

We were as lost as a pile of railroad ties
clustered in the summer sun,
splintering
splintering
splintering,
frustrated in their crossed-over lean-to position
of disuse.

We were as trapped as that rusty red subway car
abandoned where terminal tracks seek refuge under weeds,
bury themselves under the blue stone,
take commuter ghosts no further home.

————Christine Zabrouski

Penn Station II

—————Sandra Tepper Sgarro

Contributors

"I am very suspicious of people who don't take the subway."

————Richard Kostelanetz

Jeanette Adams — Jeanette Adams is the author and publisher of *Sukari, Picture Me In A Poem*, and *Love Lyrics*. She holds the MA in Creative Writing from CCNY, and has been a guest on the Poet's Corner, WFDU-FM radio.

Ren Adams — Ren Adams is a commuter who writes poems on receipts, bookmarks, scraps of paper, and yes, train tickets. She works as an editor for TrustBenefits in Emeryville and must balance the corporate madness with poetry, pirates, and video games. Ren has had poems appear in *Atom Mind, Java Snob, Poetry Motel,* among others and is working on her first book. She studied under cycle-ridin' Thom Gunn at UC Berkeley.

Abdellah Akhdi — Abdellah Akhdi is a visual artist originally from Casablanca. He has had shows in Switzerland and at the Pen & Brush Club, Salon d'Afrique and Charas en El Bohio in New York City.

Jack Anderson — Jack Anderson, a poet and dance writer, has published nine books of poetry and seven books on dance. His most recent volume of poetry, *Traffic: New and Selected Prose Poems* (New Rivers Press), won the 1998 Marie Alexander Award for prose poetry.

David Baker — David Baker is the author of eight books, most recently *Changeable Thunder* (poems, 2001), and *Heresy and the Ideal: On Contemporary Poetry* (criticism, 2000). He is poetry editor of *The Kenyon Review*, and teaches at Denison University.

Jean Balderston — Jean Balderston is a psychotherapist who lives and works in New York City. Her work has appeared in a number of literary magazines and anthologies, most recently in *Visiting Emily: Poems inspired by the Life and Work of Emily* Dickinson (University of Iowa Press). Her poem, "Dickinson Weather," was co-winner of The Poetry Society of America's *The Writer Magazine*/Emily Dickinson Award for 2000.

Lenore Balliro — Lenore Balliro is the editor of *Field Notes*, a publication for adult literary practitioners in Massachusetts. Her poetry has appeared in *minnesota review, Atlanta Review, Red Cedar Review , Clackamas Literary Review,* and elsewhere. She lives with her partner and daughter in Brookline, Mass.

Stanley H. Barkan	Stanley H. Barkan is the editor/publisher of the Cross-Cultural Review Series of World Literature & Art. In 1991, Poets House and the NYC Board of Education awarded him Poetry Teacher of the Year. His bilingual collections include, *Pàssuli cu mènnuli / Raisins with Almonds* (Sicily, 2002), *Bubbemeises & Babbaluci* (Sicily, 2001), and *Under the Apple Tree / Pod jablonia* (Kraków, 1998).
Joe Benevento	Joe Benevento teaches creative writing, literature and Spanish at Truman State U. in Kirksville, MO. His poetry, fiction and essays have appeared in over two hundred places, including: *St. Anthony Messenger, Bilingual Review,* and *Poets & Writers.* He is author of two books of poems, *Holding On* (Warthog Press, 1996) and *Willing to Believe* (Timberline Press, 2003) and the novel *Plumbing in Harlem* (PublishAmerica, 2003). He is co-editor of the *Green Hills Literary Lantern>*
Adam Berlin	Adam Berlin has a first novel published, *Headlock* (Chapel Hill: Algonquin Books, 2000) and poetry and fiction in several literary journals, including: *Santa Barbara Review, Troubador, Puerto Del Sol, Aethlon, Other Voices, Northwest Review, Notre Dame Review* and the *Bilingual Review.* He has had two nominations for Pushcart Prizes.
Linda Bosson	Linda Bosson grew up mainly in Australia but has lived for many years in New York, where she is an editor. Her poetry has appeared in publications including *Green Mountains Review, Midwest Poetry Review, The Kit-Cat Review* and *Writer's Digest.*
David Breitkopf	David Breitkopf is a writer who has worked in almost all the genres, poetry, fiction, plays, stand-up comedy and journalism. Presently he is finishing up his first novel and he is employed as a reporter for the American Banker.
Josephine Bridges	Josephine Bridges has published two poetry collections: a set of postcards and a book called *The Only Word There Is.* A native of New England, she lives in Portland, Oregon where she works as a freelance journalist; and in Blagoreshchensk, the Russian Far East, where she teaches English. She is writing a new collection of poetry and a novel, both about Russia.

W.E. Butts   W. E. Butts is the author of *A Season of Crows* (Igneus Press, 2000), and *Movies in a Small Town* (Mellen Press, 1997). He has published poems in such magazines as *Atlanta Review, Cimarron Review, Mid-American Review,* and *Poet Lore,* and has received a Pushcart Prize nomination.

Charlotte Butzin   Charlotte Butzin is an Associate Editor at *Bon Appétit* magazine. She lives in Los Angeles.

Jorge Ignacio Cortiñas   Jorge Ignacio Cortiñas awards include first prize in the 1998 Bay Guardian Fiction Contest; "playwright of the year" in *El Nuevo Herald's* 1999 year-end list; the 1999 James Assatly Memorial Prize; the 2000 Beth Lisa Feldman Prize; first prize in the 2001 Southwest Festival of New Latino Plays hosted by Stages Repertory Theatre in Houston; and a NEA / TCG supported residency with New World Theatre in Amherst.

S. Robert Crockett   S. Robert Crockett says: Rather than reading on the train, "read" the train: fantasy playing across Manhattan's marvelous mosaic of passengers, physical details leading to associations through the magic of metaphor, lifting consciousness to that archetypal level where myth makes us all Celebrants of Life.

Enid Dame   Enid Dame is a poet, Brooklynite, and frequent subway rider. Her books of poems include *Lilith and Her Demons,* (Cross-Cultural Communications) and *Anything You Don't See* (West End). She co-edits *Home Planet News* with Donald Lev and teaches at New Jersey Institute of Technology and Rutgers University. She is co-editor of the anthology *Which Lilith? Feminist Writers Re-Create the World's First Woman* (Jason Aronson).

Kathryn Daniels   Kathryn Daniels is a poet and fiction writer living in New York City. Her work has appeared in numerous publications including the anthologies *If I Had a Hammer* (Papier Mache Press) and *Boomer Girls* (University of Iowa Press).

Robin Dann   A multimedia artist from Brooklyn, Rabin Dann is a work in progress. Currently, she is working on a novel and a series of interactive installations, among other projects.

Nina Drooker	Nina Drooker, a retired New York City schoolteacher, is a poet, a painter, and a student of art history at Hunter College. Her poems have been published in *Slant, Global City Review, Exit 13, Home Planet News*, and the *Jewish Women's Literary Annual*.
George Drury	George Drury's work is included on a CD released in Köln presenting a soundscape which captures "the cadences of the manifold branching out of the special day to day culture of Chicago."
Lonnie Hull DuPont	Lonnie Hull DuPont lives in rural Michigan where she is a freelance book editor, writer of biographies for young readers and a poet. Her poems have appeared most recently in *Haight Ashbury Literary Journal, Americas Review* and in the 1999 University of Iowa poetry anthology, *Boomer Girls*, now in its fourth printing. She is the author of *The Haiku Box* (Tuttle Publishing, 2001) and five poetry chapbooks.
Maureen Tolman Flannery	Maureen Tolman Flannery , author of *Secret of the Rising UP: Poems of Mexico* and *Remembered Into Life*, has edited *Knowing Stones: Poems of Exotic Places*. Raised on a Wyoming ranch, she lives in Chicago with her actor husband Dan and their four wonderful children. Her poems have appeared in over a hundred literary journals and anthologies, including *Atlanta Review, Mid America Poetry Review*, and *Woven on the Wind*.
Adrian Robert Ford	Adrian Robert Ford, 55, has lived in Chicago for 30 years but was raised in the Finger Lakes. He collects contemporary Japanese prints and admires the international minimalist aesthetic.
Cynthia Gallaher	Cynthia Gallaher, aficionado of Chicago, New York and London subways, author of *Night Ribbons* (Polar Bear Press), *Swimmer's Prayer* (Missing Spoke Press) and *Earth Elegance* (March / Abrazo Press), dreams nearly nightly of train travel. She was recently placed on the Chicago Library's "Top Ten" list of requested Chicago poets. Look for new work in *Stand Up Poetry An Expanded Anthology* (University of Iowa Press, 2002).
Ryn Gargulinski	Ryn Gargulinski is a poet, journalist, cartoonist, and humorist. Her work, which ranges from haiku to a thesis on Folklore of New York City Subway

Workers, has appeared in various publications. Her monthly Brooklyn column can be found online at www.12gauge.com.

Peggy Garrison Peggy Garrison teaches creative writing workshops at NYU; she is also a writer-in-residence for Teachers & Writers Collaborative. Her most recent poetry chapbooks are *Charing Cross Bridge* (P&Q Press) and *Ding the Bell* (Poetry New York) in collaboration with artist, Lesley Heathcote. Her work has appeared in a number of literary magazines, among them *South Dakota Review*, *Poetry New York*, *Global City Review*, *Mudfish* and *Home Planet News*.

John Gilgun John Gilgun is the author of *Everything That Has Been Shall Be Again: The Reincarnation Fables of John Gilgun*, (Bieler Press, 1981); *Music I Never Dreamed Of* (Amethyst Press, 1989); *From the Inside Out* (Three Phase, 1991); *The Dooley Poems* (Robin Price, 1991); *In the Zone: The Moby Dick Poems* (Pecan Grove Press, 2002) and *Your Buddy Misses You* (Three Phase, 1995).

Robin M. Glassman Brooklyn artist, Robin M. Glassman creates ink drawings to capture her daily commute on MTA's "F" train. For over 25 years she has explored her internal and external experiences through drawing and a variety of other media including watercolor, collage and recycled polystyrene-based sculpture. Glassman is a member of Brooklyn Working Artists Coalition. She is the creator, designer, illustrator and publisher of *ILLUMINATIONS: An Alphabet Book to Color and Healing*.

Tony Gloeggler Tony Gloeggler currently manages a group home for developmentally disabled young men in Brooklyn. His work has appeared in *West Branch, New York Quarterly, Rattle, Graffiti Rag, The Ledge* and *Puerto del Sol*. His chapbook, *One on One*, was named winner of the 1998 Pearl Poetry Prize and his first book, *One Wish Left*, will be published by Pavement Saw Press in 2002.

Eve Goodman Eve Goodman, Bronx native, left New York after 25 years, a good part of that time spent on subways, which still crop up in her dreams. Occasionally some of her poems and stories appear in magazines. She is currently attempting a novel.

Piotr Gwiazda	Piotr Gwiazda teaches English and American literature at the University of Miami in Coral Gables. His poems have recently appeared in *Columbia: A Journal of Literature and Art*, *Rattle*, and *Washington Square*.
Steven Hartman	Steven Hartman is a poet-collage-artist-accountant who lives four subway stops from Coney Island. A nominee of Downtown Magazine Poet-of-the-Year in 1996, he has had poems published in *Atom Mind*, *Coffeehouse Poetry Anthology*, *Slipstream* and The *New York Daily News* and performed on WBAI and at the Saint Mark's Poetry Project, Jackie 60 and Amos Eno Gallery. He is the author of two chapbooks: *Pinched Nerves* (Cross-Cultural Communications) and *Coffeebreak Poems* (Trout Creek Press).
George Held	George Held, the author of three poetry chapbooks, has a book of poems forthcoming from Cedar Hill. He has lived in Greenwich Village and taught English at Queens College since 1967.
Corie Herman	Corie Herman earned her MFA from New York University and is a Poet-in-Residence in NYC public schools. She was a finalist in the 2000 Randall Jarrell Poetry and the 1998 Sue Saniel Elkind Poetry Prizes. Her work has appeared in *Kalliope*, *Calyx*, *Natural Bridge*, *So to Speak*, and *Phoebe*. Her first collection of poems, *Radishes Into Roses*, was published by Linear Arts Press.
Carlos Hernandez	Carlos Hernandez was born in 1971 in Aurora, Illinois. He graduated with a Ph.D. in English/Creative Writing from Binghamton University in 2000. He has published poetry, short stories and plays in a variety of places, including *Happy*, *Flashquake*, *The Paterson Literary Review*, *Slant*, *Sun Dog* and *The Muse Apprentice Guild*. He lives in Queens, NY and directs the First-Year Students program at Pace University.
Jill Hoffman	Jill Hoffman is the author of *Black Diaries*, poems (Box Turtle Press), 2000; *Jilted*, a novel (Simon and Schuster), 1993; and *Mink Coat*, poems (Holt, Rinehart & Winston), 1973. She was awarded a Guggenheim Fellowship in Poetry and holds degrees from Bennington, and Columbia, and a Ph.D. from Cornell. She teaches a writing workshop in Tribeca, and at The New School, and is the founding editor of *Mudfish*.

Pud Houstoun	Pud Houstoun – Painter and poet. BFA, winner of Joe and Emily Lowe Award; exhibition at the Ward Eggleston Gallery, New York; recent recipient of grant from the Pollock-Krasner Foundation. Her poems have appeared in *Midwest Poetry Review, Frogpond, Modern Haiku, Bottle Rockets*, and *Potpourri*.
Walida Imarisha	Author of the chapbook "children of ex-slaves: the unfinished revolution," Walidah Imarisha is a poet, journalist, activist, historian and general rabble rouser currently based in Philadelphia. She is one half of the poetry dynamic duo Good Sista/Bad Sista with her partner in rhyme Turiya Autry. The two toured the country summer 2001 with their power packed performance poetry.
Jacqueline Jules	Jacqueline Jules is the author of two children's books, *The Grey Striped Shirt* and *Once Upon a Shabbos*. Her poetry and prose has or will appear in over sixty publications including *America, Cricket, Cicada, Cape Rock, Capper's, Small Pond Magazine, Echoes, Class, Lullwater Review, Potomac Review, Chaminade Literary Review, Plastic Tower, Oxalis, Santa Barbara Review, Skylark, Rain Dog Review, Sow's Ear Review, Minimus, Psychopoetica, Mobius, Northern Reader*, and *Sunstone*. She was a 1999 winner in the Arlington County Moving Words Competition.
Stephen Kaplan	Stephen Kaplan has lived in New York all his life and seen the subways and els go through many changes. He has had poems published in *On the Bus, Poetry Motel* and others forthcoming. He is a painter as well and the recipient of a Pollock-Krasner foundation grant.
Kit Kennedy	Kit Kennedy's work has appeared in *Phoebe, Haight Ashbury Literary Journal, Manzanita Quarterly*, the anthology *GRRRRR*, among others. She lives in San Francisco and works in sales. She lived in NYC for ten years and rode the Broadway local.
Thomas Krampf	Thomas Krampf lives in Hinsdale, NY with his wife, Françoise. He has three grown daughters and grandchildren. He is the author of three books of poems, *Subway Prayer and Other Poems of the Inner City, Satori West*, and *Shadow Poems*.

A fourth manuscript, *Poems of Madness*, is forthcoming. He recently returned from a month of giving poetry workshops in Ireland. He still misses the subway.

Joyce Kravets
Joyce Kravets writes poetry and stories as well as recollections of growing up in a Holocaust survivor community. A psychotherapist, a grandmother and a work-out addict, her writing group calls her a literary crone with muscle tone.

Otis Kriegel
Otis Kriegel is a public school teacher, who has taught in both New York City and Los Angeles He now teaches first grade in San Francisco. He is currently working on his first play.

Donna J. Gelagotis Lee
Donna J. Gelagotis Lee has poetry published or forthcoming in *The Bitter Oleander, CALYX, A Journal of Art and Literature by Women, The Cortland Review, Hurricane Alice, The Midwest Quarterly*, and *Wisconsin Review*. She has just completed her first book, *The Draw of Time*. She is currently finishing a second poetry manuscript, entitled *On the Altar of* Greece. Donna is a freelance editor in New Jersey.

Rosalyn S. Lee
Rosalyn S. Lee is a 46-year-old African American New Yorker who is an architectural designer by day and writes short stories, poetry and creates graphic arts at night. She is published in two anthologies and is currently working on her novel.

Donald Lev
Donald Lev has been writing and publishing poetry for over forty years. His twelfth collection is *Enemies of Time* (Warthog Press, 2000). Since 1979, he and his wife, Enid Dame, have been co-editing the literary tabloid *Home Planet News*.

Lyn Lifshin
Lyn Lifshin's most recent prize-winning book, (Paterson poetry award) *Before It's Light*, was published by Black Sparrow press (2000). She has published more than 100 books of poetry including *Marilyn Monroe, Blue Tattoo*, edited 4 anthologies of women's writing including *Tangled Vines, Ariadne's Thread* and *Lips Unsealed*. Her poems have appeared in most literary and poetry magazines and she is the subject of an award winning documentary film, *Lyn Lifshin: Not Made of Glass*, (Women Make Movies).

Susan Mahan	Susan Mahan has been writing poetry since her husband died in 1997. She is a frequent reader at poetry venues and has written two chap books, "Paris Awaits" and "In The Wilderness of Grief". She recently joined the editorial staff of <u>The South Boston Literary Gazette</u> and is a recent member of the South Boston Arts Association.
D. H. Melhem	D. H. Melhem, Ph.D., is the author of five books of poetry, one novel, two critical works including the first comprehensive study of Gwendolyn Brooks, a musical drama (*Children of the House Afire*, produced 1999), a creative writing book, over fifty essays, and has edited three anthologies. Winner of numerous awards, she serves as vice-president of the International Women's Writing Guild.
Jose Luis Mojica	Jose Luis Mojica is a cartoonist/illustrator currently working as an art director. He has illustrated two stories for *Strange Behaviors, a comic book* (Twilight Tone Press, March 2001), and has just been accepted as a story board artist for film at Famous Frames.
Gertrude Morris	Gertrude Morris has had work in many publications, including: *Film Library Quarterly, Waterways* (about 80 poems), *Midstream, Mind The Gap, Rattapallax,* (CD and Weblinks), *Anthology of Magazine Verse & Yearbook of American Poetry 1997, Modern Haiku, frogpond, Haiku Headlines, Timepieces.* Poems upcoming in *Mudfish* 13. She has also received awards for her poetry and grants from Poets & Writers, Inc. for teaching Poetry Workshops, readings and for an original play
Lillian Morrison	Lillian Morrison is the author of a number of poetry books, among them, *The Ghosts of Jersey City Overheard in a Bubble* Chamber and most recently *Way to Go! Sports Poems.* Her anthology *More Spice Than Sugar; Poems about Feisty Females* will be published by Houghton Mifflin in February, 2001. Single poems have appeared in *Confrontation, The Listening Eye, Poetry Northwest* and other periodicals.
Shin Yu Pai	Shin Yu Pai has published poems, translations, and photographs in *580 Split, Mungo vs. Ranger, Bostonia,* and *Eye.Caramba.com.* A chapbook of Chinese poetic translations is available through

	Third Ear Books. Her one act play *Concave is the Opposite of Convex* was read last year in the *Where Theater Starts Reading Series* sponsored by The Hudson Exploited Theater Company.
Brent Pallas	Brent Pallas has lived in New York for 20 years. His most recent poems have appeared in *Poetry, Poetry Northwest,* and *Rattapallax.*
Lance Peterson	Lance Peterson has published in the *Hawaii Review, The Nerve Bundle Review. The Sounds of Poetry, Psychopoetica,* and the *HazMat Review.* With an MA in English from SUNY Binghamton he is currently teaching at Broome County Community College.
David Quintavalle	David Quintavalle writes fiction and poetry while traveling to and from his home in Greenwich Village and his work in the midtown financial district. His poetry has appeared in *Slant, Mudfish, CQ, modern words, Gulfstream, Home Planet News* and *Global City Review.* His chapbooks, *Inky Star* and *The Carl Chronicles* were published by P&Q Press
Lola Rodriguez	Lola Rodriguez was chosen by Los Angeles' *Latin Beat Magazine* as one of the most important women in the arts today. Her work is featured in the books, *The Coffeehouse Poetry Anthology, Poets and Painters, New to North America, A Millenium Journal, For the Lives of Us;* and in the journals, *The Columbia Review, Barrow Street, Calyx* and *American Mensa Wordfun,* etc. Rodriguez was recently nominated for the Pushcart Prize.
w. r. rodriguez	w. r. rodriguez is the author of *the shoe shine parlor poems et al*, narratives and lyrics of the South Bronx. Recently he has completed its sequel, *the concrete pastures of the beautiful bronx.*
William Pitt Root	William Pitt Root's *Trace Elements From a Recurring Kingdom* (1994) recollected his first five books, more current work appears in *Commonweal, Manoa, Poetry International, Whole Earth, Orpheus & Company, And What Rough Beast,* etc. Recently he represented the US at poetry festivals in Malmo Sweden and Macedonia. Root lives in Tuscson and teaches in the Hunter College MFA program.

Sue Rosen	Sue Rosen has an M.S. from Florida International University. She studied creative writing at the University of Miami and is currently teaching writing at The New School. Publications include *A Literary Day* , (P&Q Press), poetry in numerous small press publications and creative nonfiction in *The Appalachian Women's Journal, The Charleston Gazette, The Sun Sentinel, The Miami Herald* and *The Jackson Herald*.
sandra tepper	We regret that sandra died January 2003.
sgarro	Exhibitions and Awards: Pen and Brush Holiday Show/Kathe Berle Memorial Award, Donnell Small Works Exhibit, NYC/Merit Award, Plainfield Art Festival, NJ, Highland Park 2000 Photo Exhibit.
David Sanua	David Sanua practices workers' compensation law (Kafka's specialty) out of his basement in Brooklyn. His poem *The Terminus Station*, a seven-page subway epic, was publised in the summer 1998 issue of the *Cardozo Studies in Law and Literature*.
D. David Sapp`	David Sapp's poems have appeared in *The Chattahoochee Review, The Bad Henry Review, The Dirty Goat, Sidewalks, The Cape Rock, Meat Whistle Quarterly, Mad Poets Review, Open Bone Review, The Heartlands Today*, and elsewhere. He lives and teaches in Ohio near Lake Erie.
Myra Shapiro	Myra Shapiro, born in the Bronx, returned to NYC after 45 years in Georgia and Tennessee. Her work has appeared in periodicals and anthologies, most recently *Bronx Accent* (Rutgers University Press, 2000) and *The Best American Poetry of 1999*. She serves on the board of Poets House and teaches workshops for the International Woman's Writers' Guild. Her book, *I'll See You Thursday*, was published by Blue Sofa Press in 1996.
Susan Sherman	Susan Sherman is the former editor of IKON magazine. She lives and writes in New York City.
Dan Sicoli	Dan Sicoli is co-founder and co-editor of *Slipstream Magazine and Press*. Cars, broken guitar strings, party dresses, and coffee beans have often made their way into his poetry. Pudding House Publications recently released his chapbook, *Pagan Supper*. Recent web e-zine credits include *Atomic Petals, Bulkhead, 2River View, American Poetry Consortium, Opium* and *Erosha*. He also makes his own sausage.

Dan Sieg	Dan Sieg, born and raised in Detroit, is employed as a senior therapist at a family and children's clinic in the Bronx. He was educated at Wayne State and Adelphi University. Previous poems have appeared in *Small Brushes, Blueline Press , Mobius, G.W. Review, Voices International, West Hills Review, The Iconoclast* and elsewhere.
Elizabeth Simson	Elizabeth Simson's work appears or is forthcoming in *Earth's Daughters, Sagewoman, Gertrude, The Blue Moon Review, Mentress Moon* and elsewhere. Her poetry was published in the anthologies <u>2001: A Science Fiction Poetry Anthology</u> (Editor's Choice Award, Anamnesis Press) and <u>Earth Beneath, Sky Beyond</u> (Outrider Press). She earned her BA from Willamette University and received the Younger Scholar's Award from the National Endowment for the Humanities.
Ian Thal	Ian Thal is a Washington, D.C. born, Boston based poet, pantomimist, performance artist, critic, and rail fan who has performed throughout the northeastern United States. His poems and book reviews have appeared in *Poesy, Ibbetson Street Press, Crooked River Press* and *The Jewish Advocate*. He is a member of the Cosmic Spelunker Theater, a multi-generational performance troupe featuring both poetry and pantomime.
Vincent J. Tomeo	Vincent J. Tomeo has 108 poems published in anthologies, magazines newspapers, and a tape *The Sound of Poetry*; awarded honorable mention in the 1999 Ranier Maria Rilke International Poetry Competition; and fourth place in the Sky Blue Poetry League's 2001 contest. He has a publication in braille, *Whispers from the Heart in the Darkness on the Floor*, published by International Lighthouse Press, 1999. He has presented several poetry readings at various libraries in New York City.
Nikki Tommins	Nikki Tommins grew up in Newark New Jersey. Her play, "Pumpkin Seeds" will be performed in Montclair New Jersey, where she is a member of New Voices, women's writing forum. Other publications include *The 13th Story, Crimescribe* and *Boardwalk Magazine*.

Meneba Obasai Tresk	Meneba Obasai Tresk, aka Lawrence Zabrieskie, is a caustic poet and writer living in Clinton Hill, Brooklyn. He holds a B.A. from New York University. He has read his works at many venues, including the Harlem Theatre Company, Medgar Evers College, NYU, and The Three Jewels Bookstore. Recently, Three Jewels published their own anthology entitled "Three Jewels: Selected Poets", which featured twenty of Obasai's poems. Feel free to email him at: menebatresk@aol.com
Michael Waters	Michael Waters teaches at Salisbury University on the Eastern Shore of Maryland. Recent books include *Parthenopi: New and Selected Poems* (BOA Editions, 2001) and, with the late A. Poulin, Jr., the Seventh Edition of *Contemporary American Poetry* (Houghton Mifflin, 2001). In 2002, Southern Illinois University Press will publish *Perfect in Their Art: Poems on Boxing from Homer to Ali*, edited with Robert Hedin.
Patricia Wild	Patricia Wild, a twenty-year resident of Somerville, MA. is the author of *Swimming In It*, a novel set in Somerville, published in 1999 by Flower Valley Press, Inc. A columnist for the *Somerville Journal*, she's presently completing the sequel to her first book.
Christine A. Zabrouski	Christine A. Zabrouski was born and raised in Queens, New York. She has written four books of poetry, not yet published: *Flatline, A Ton of Feathers, One Wish* and *Where's My White Picket Fence?* She has a Bachelor's Degree in Communication Arts from Queens College and is currently working towards a degree in photography. Christine currently works in Public Relations for St. Mary's in Manhasset, New York.

This page constitutes
an extension of the copyright page.

"Ghosts", by Lonnie Hull DuPont, first appeared in *Haight Ashbury Literary Journal*, Vol. 15, # 11. Copyright © 1996 by Lonnie Hull DuPont and reprinted with her permission.

"El Exchange," by Maureen Tolman Flannery, first appeared in *Sport Literate*, "Issue of the Big Shoulders," Vol. 3, Iss. 1, (1999). Copyright © 1999 by Maureen Tolman Flannery and reprinted with her permission.

"B Station," by Cynthia Gallaher, from her book *Swimmer's Prayer* (Seattle WA: Missing Spoke Press, 1999). Copyright © 1999 by Cynthia Gallaher and reprinted with her permission.

"A Subway Ride in New York," by Peggy Garrison, first appeared in *The Green Hills Literary Lantern*. Copyright © 2002 by Peggy Garrison and reprinted with her permission.

"Subway Pocket Poem," by Tony Gloeggler, first appeared in *Wisconsin Review*, Vol. 34 , Iss. 2, (Winter 2000). Copyright © 1999 by Tony Gloeggler and reprinted with his permission.

"Motion" and "At the Subway in Grand Central Stations," by Carlos Hernandez from his poem "For Milt", first appeared in *Patterson Literary Review*, Iss. #31, (2001). Copyright © 2001 Carlos Hernandez and reprinted with his permission.

"Manhattan Community College", by Jill Hoffman, first appeared in *black diaries* (New York, NY: Box Turtle Press, 2000). Copyright © 2000 by Jill Hoffman and reprinted with her permission.

"A Prayer to the Subway," by Thomas Krampf, *Subway Prayer and Other Poems of the Inner City* (Morning Star Press, 1976). Copyright © 1976 b y Thomas Krampf and reprinted with his permission. Originally published in *The Phoenix Literary Quarterly,* Vol. IV, No. 1, (Jan 1973).

"The Passenger," by Donald Lev, first appeared in *There is Still Time* (Providence, RI: The Poet's Press, 1986). Copyright © 1986 by Donald Lev and reprinted with his permission.

"subway," by D. H. Melhem, from her book *Children of the House Afire* (Dovetail Press, 1976). Copyright © 1976 by D. H. Melhem and reprinted with her permission.

"Miss Subways," by Gertrude Morris, first appeard in *Waterways* (April 1995). Copyright © 1995 by Gertrude Morris and reprinted with her permission.

"The A Train," by Lillian Morrison, from her book *The Break Dance Kids* (Lothrop, Lee & Shepard, 1985). Copyright © 1985 by Lillian Morrison and reprinted with her permission.

"Transience," by Shin Yu Pai, first appeared in *Mungo vs. Ranger* (Fall Issue, 1999). Copyright © 1999 by Shin Yu Pai and reprinted with her permission.

"Underground", by Lance Peterson, first appeared in *HazMat Review*, Vol 3, Iss. 2. Copyright © 1998 by Lance Peterson and reprinted with his permission.

"The A Train," by David Quintavalle, first appeared in *The Green Hills Literary Lantern* (Fall Issue, 2001). Copyright © 2001 b y David Quintavalle and reprinted with his permission.

"Gold in the Subway," by Myra Shapiro, first appeared in *The Worcester Review*, Vol XXI, No. 1 & 2. Copyright © 2000 by Myra Shapiro and reprinted with her permission.

"tuesday," by Dan Sicoli, first appeared in *Third Lung Review*, Iss. # 2, (Summer 1987). Copyright © 1987 by Dan Sicoli and reprinted with his permission.

"Into the Station," by Ian Thal, first appeared in *Poesy: A Publication for Poetry and the Arts*, Iss. 12, (Spring 2001). Copyright © 2001 by Ian Thal and reprinted with his permission.

"The '66 Mets," by Michael Waters, from his book *Parthenopi: New and Selected Poems* (BOA Editions: 2001). Copyright © 1993 by Michael Waters and reprinted with his permission. Originally published in *The Missouri Review*, Vol.XXI, No. 1, (1993).

Other Publications from P&Q Press

Book design by David Quintavalle

Cover photograph by David Quintavalle

Cover design by Jim Millefolie & David Quintavalle

Text: Georgia

Printed by